Kimon Friar and Nikos Kazantzakis

KIMON FRIAR
The Spiritual Odyssey of Nikos Kazantzakis

A TALK

EDITED AND WITH AN INTRODUCTION BY
Theofanis G. Stavrou

The First Annual Public Lecture
    in Modern Greek Studies
    Special Collections
    University of Minnesota Libraries
    Minneapolis

The North Central Publishing Company
1979

Copyright © 1979 Nostos
ALL RIGHTS RESERVED

Library of Congress Card Number: 79-90836

ISBN 0-935476-00-8

The publication of this volume was made possible with assistance from Nostos, the Society for the Study of Greek Life and Thought, Minneapolis, Minnesota

Cover photograph of Nikos Kazantzakis taken by Kimon Friar, Summer 1954.
Frontispiece photograph of Nikos Kazantzakis and Kimon Friar taken by Helen Kazantzakis.
Centerpiece "Homage to Homer: The Return of Ulysses" by Salvador Dali. Courtesy of Theofanis G. Stavrou.

TABLE OF CONTENTS

INTRODUCTION, 1

THE SPIRITUAL ODYSSEY
OF NIKOS KAZANTZAKIS, 9

SUPPLEMENT

A FEW LETTERS FROM NIKOS KAZANTZAKIS
TO KIMON FRIAR, 33

CRITICAL COMMENT ON THE
ODYSSEY: A MODERN SEQUEL, 39

INTRODUCTION

This small volume is a tribute to the best known of modern Greek writers, Nikos Kazantzakis (1883–1957) and his major work the *Odyssey* which some critics have described as the single most ambitious literary accomplishment of the twentieth century. At the same time, the volume is a tribute to Kimon Friar, poet, translator and friend of Kazantzakis who by translating the *Odyssey* into English freed it from the confines of the Greek-speaking world. In a way it is also a tribute to the remarkable collaboration which went beyond mere translation to the recreation of this monumental literary work.[1] Finally, it is a tribute to Basil Laourdas (1912–1971), a neohellenist, who was among the first to preoccupy himself as a critic with Kazantzakis' work, especially the *Odyssey*. The occasion that led to this published tribute was the dedication of the Basil Laourdas Modern Greek Collection on May 19, 1978 under the sponsorship of Special Collections of the O. Meredith Wilson Library at the University of Minnesota.[2]

---

[1] The story of this collaboration is told by Kimon Friar himself in "A Unique Collaboration: Translating *The Odyssey: A Modern Sequel*," *Journal of Modern Literature (Nikos Kazantzakis Special Number)*, 2. 2 (1971–1972):215–244.

[2] Basil Laourdas' valuable modern Greek collection was donated to the University of Minnesota by Mrs. Louisa Laourdas. It will be cared for by Special Collections of the University and it will serve as a nucleus for developing a research library in the intellectual and cultural history of modern Greece. This corresponds with the interests of Basil Laourdas who until his death sought to promote modern Greek studies outside Greece. For a brief description of the Laourdas collection see Theofanis G. Stavrou, *Vivliothiki Vasili Laourda* (The Library of Basil Laourdas), published by Special Collections, O. Meredith Wilson Library, University of Minnesota, 1978, on the occasion of the dedication of this collection. I wish to acknowledge the cooperation and contribution of a number of individuals who made this event possible. First of all, Mrs. Louisa Laourdas who donated the collection and who flew from Greece for the occasion; my colleague Professor Clarke Chambers who, as Chairman of the History Department, negotiated the arrangements for bringing the collection to the University of Minnesota; Mr. Eldred Smith, who as Director of the University Libraries, officially accepted the collection; Mr. C. Peter Magrath, President of the University, who addressed the more than 200 member audience of University officials, professors, students and members of the community; Professor Michael C. Petrovich of the History De-

Nikos Kazantzakis has a way of taking hold of his readers as if by a storm. He invites them to participate in a spiritual as well as intellectual exercise, and inevitably those who study him carefully become possessed by his "Cretan glance." They are fascinated by his spiritual struggle for "freedom," even from freedom itself, which characterized his entire life, and by the range of his ceaseless and diverse creative activity which cast him as a person of prodigious will. This constant struggle, by which Kazantzakis expected man to surpass his natural limitations, characterized his existence as a human being and as a writer, and is felt deeply by his readers. All who got to know him speak and write about the "appeal" of Kazantzakis' personality: his commitment to the "struggle," his sense of mission, his dedication, his erudition, his insatiable curiosity and thirst for knowledge, his acceptance and rejection of all sorts of political and religious creeds, his numerous wanderings, his hermetic proclivities, his passion for the triumph of the Greek demotic language, and above all his industry without which there would be no Kazantzakis question today. In short, he was an "uncompromising" individual, as his wife Helen suggests by so referring to him in the title of her recently published biography, or an "irregular verb" as Kazantzakis himself was fond of describing himself.[3] This fascination with Kazantzakis' personality and work may be partly due to the fact that Kazantzakis "belongs more to the general history of culture than to the narrow

---

partment, University of Wisconsin, Madison, who spoke on "Basil Laourdas: Scholar and Friend;" and the keynote speaker, Mr. Kimon Friar, who spoke on "The Spiritual Odyssey of Nikos Kazantzakis." I wish to acknowledge in a special way the contributions of Mr. Austin McLean, Chief of Special Collections and his colleagues, Mr. John Jenson and Ms. Kathy Tezla, who mounted an ambitious but elegant book exhibit in connection with the event and which remained opened from May 19 to July 31, 1978. Finally, my thanks to students and friends of modern Greek culture who demonstrated by their attendance that there is a strong interest in modern Greek studies at the University of Minnesota. The publication of this volume is, among other things, a small contribution in the efforts to sustain an active interest in this field.

[3] The reference is to the title of the Greek edition (*Nikos Kazantzakis: The Uncompromising Man*, Athens, 1977) of Helen Kazantzakis, *Nikos Kazantzakis A Biography* (New York: Simon and Schuster, 1968). This is the impression conveyed by most biographers of Kazantzakis beginning with the most responsible of them all, Pandelis Prevelakis. See his *Nikos Kazantzakis and His Odyssey: A Study of the Poet and the Poem* translated by Philip Sherrard with a preface by Kimon Friar (New York: Simon and Schuster, 1961; Greek edition, Athens, 1958). Those interested further in Kazantzakis should consult the useful "Kazantzakis Check List" by Peter Bien in *Mandatophoros Bulletin of Modern Greek Studies*, Special Issue (November 1974), and the more accessible one by Donald Falconio, "Critics of Kazantzakis: Selected Checklist of Writings in English," *Journal of Modern Literature* 2.2 (1971–1972):314–326. A forthcoming translation by Theodora

limits of modern Greek literature," as Constantine Dhimaras has suggested.[4]

It is easy to detect immediately a certain internationalism in the life and work of Kazantzakis, the result of his study and travels abroad, especially Europe. In a strange way for a person who has been variously described as a "loner," an "outsider," an "alienated intellectual," a "desperado," Kazantzakis was remarkably cosmopolitan, moving comfortably from one cultural milieu to another, simultaneously studying them passionately. Still, he never forsook his Cretan and, by extension, his Greek heritage. He would most frequently transcend it or, as a true "intelligent," subject it to ruthless examination and criticism, expose the abuses and failings of some of its institutions, and wish for its purging and revitalization, but invariably he would return to it for inspiration and reassurance. It constituted part of his "Cretan glance," his world view. This problematization and attempt at reconciliation between, among other things, tradition and modernity, Europe and Asia, rationalism and emotion, the Apollonian and the Dionysian, extreme individualism and "collective dreams" account for the immediate response that Kazantzakis exacted and continues to exact from his readers, Greeks or non-Greeks.

It is also easy to detect that everything Kazantzakis had undertaken as a man and as a writer until the eve of the Second World War pointed toward the *Odyssey* in which he emptied himself of all his visions about his and twentieth-century man's existential concerns. His correspondence, especially with his best

---

Vasils of Nikos Kazantzakis, *Serpent and Lily* (Berkeley: University of California Press), includes a bibliography of works by Kazantzakis available in English.

The twentieth anniversary of Kazantzakis' death in October 1977, provided the occasion for the appearance of a number of works, some original, others reflective, by individuals who knew him personally and who in some way or other were influenced by him. These accounts, too, convey the impression about Kazantzakis mentioned above. Notable among these new accounts are: *Theorisi tou Nikou Kazantzaki eikosi chronia apo to thanato tou (Review of Nikos Kazantzakis Twenty Years After His Death)*, Tetradhia "Evthinis," No. 3 (Athens, 1977), where thirteen significant figures of modern Greek letters and culture, including Pandelis Prevelakis, review the work and personality of the Cretan author, and where ten new letters of Kazantzakis to Aim. Chourmouzios are published; a special issue of *Kainouria epochi (New Epoch)* 9 (Spring 1978), dedicated to Nikos Kazantzakis; Elli Alexiou and G. Emm. Stephanakis, *Ya ton Nikon Kazantzaki eikosi chronia apo ton thanato tou (For Nikos Kazantzakis Twenty Years After His Death)* (Athens: Kedhros, 1977); and Aim. Chourmouziou, *Nikos Kazantzakis* (Athens: Ekdhoseis ton Philon, 1977), which is the fourth volume in a new edition of the celebrated critic's works.

[4] C. Th. Dimaras, *Modern Greek Literature*, translated by Mary P. Gianos (Albany: State University of New York Press, 1972), p. 455.

friend Pandelis Prevelakis, makes it abundantly clear that the *Odyssey* held first priority in his life. His numerous travels were missions for gathering facts, impressions, and symbols which filled the *Odyssey*. All his other writings were rehearsals, exercises for the big literary struggle which was the *Odyssey*. He carried it with him wherever he went, referred everything he read to it, wrote the first drafts with demonic speed but reworked them with a craftsman's patience and a prophet's conviction. It took him fourteen arduous years (1924–1938), during which time he also wrote many other works, to deliver the finished product of 33,333 verses. By any measure, the *Odyssey* is an incredible poetic achievement and, as Pandelis Prevelakis put it, "if read with the attention it deserves it is capable of changing the reader's soul."[5]

Finally, it is equally easily detectable that Kazantzakis was a profoundly spiritual writer despite his iconoclastic pronouncements about religion in general and organized religion in particular. His religious roots ran deep, and no matter how much he snipped away at them, they continued to grow to the point where all his works are permeated by a spiritual fervor. This is true of his plays, poems, novels, "philosophical" essays, even his travel accounts. It is also true that all his works reveal him as a political writer as well.

Inevitably, serious students of Kazantzakis become acquainted with the excitement and controversy which has been generated by both the life and work of the Cretan writer, a controversy which reached a critical point with the publication of the *Odyssey*. Kazantzakis expected that the Greek critics would have been impressed by his accomplishment. But whereas some praised it as an unprecedented epic, many simply viewed it as a hybristic act; Kazantzakis felt that many, if not most, Greek critics failed to understand the message of his *Odyssey*.

Among the first to study seriously Kazantzakis' epic poem was a young man by the name of Basil Laourdas. Laourdas had initially admired this huge work. In fact, for a while, he considered it as his credo. But as he pondered on the linguistic, philological, philosophical and cultural questions raised in that monumental work, what was for Laourdas a credo gradually became a problem. Laourdas' attitude toward Kazantzakis' work, especially the

---

[5] Pandelis Prevelakis, "Kazantzakis, Vios kai Ergha" (Kazantzakis' Life and Works), Tetradhia "Evthinis," No. 3 (1977):9–45. Prevelakis made this statement in his memorial address on the occasion of the twentieth anniversary of Kazantzakis' death on October 26, 1977, in the Basilica of St. Mark in Irakleion, Crete. This address is the best summary and analysis of Kazantzakis' life and work in any language, and it should be translated into English.

Odyssey, is more complex than is usually assumed. It must be remembered that Laourdas' critical essay appeared in 1943, during the German occupation of Greece. The young Laourdas was concerned with the immediate dangers facing the nation and grew impatient with Greek writers who seemed to ignore native traditions and who came instead under the influence of European ideologies. His world view and his religious and national concerns militated against his continued acceptance of the *Odyssey*, even though by 1942 Kazantzakis' hostility against, and his criticism of, modern Hellenism, which had obsessed him during the interwar years, had been gradually replaced by a peculiar "mellow nationalism" or patriotism, as reflected in his novel *Zorba the Greek*, written during the Second World War.[6] This "rejection" of the *Odyssey* has been exaggeratedly misunderstood and has been interpreted as a general rejection by Laourdas of Kazantzakis and his work.[7]

Controversy over the nature of Kazantzakis' contribution to modern Greek literature and culture will undoubtedly continue, but any discussion of modern Greek literature and thought without appropriate references to Kazantzakis is inconceivable. For to quote Dhimaras again, "At the convergence of movements and

---

[6] Laourdas' critical essay, *The Odyssey of Kazantzakis* (Athens, 1943), was reprinted in a collection of his essays, *Philologhika Dhokimia (Literary Critical Essays)*, edited and with an introduction by Dinos Christianopoulos (Thessaloniki, 1977), pp. 1–22. The best balanced account of the philosophical problems Laourdas experienced while studying the *Odyssey* is a special essay by Pandelis Prevelakis, "Mnimosino sto Vasileio Laourda" (Memorial to Basil Laourdas), included in the volume, *Essays in Memory of Basil Laourdas* (Thessaloniki, 1975), pp. 29–43. With regard to the question of Kazantzakis' return to his native roots during the Second Word War, see Basil Laourdas, "Ideas and Ideals in Contemporary Greek Literature," *Balkan Studies* 9 (1968): 155–166. Peter Bien deals with the same question in greater detail in a paper which he read at the Modern Greek Studies Association Conference in Washington, D.C. (November 11, 1978), on "Nationalism versus Patriotism in Kazantzakis' 'Occupational Novel,' *Zorba the Greek*," and which will be part of his forthcoming study on the politics of Kazantzakis.

[7] In 1966, in Thessaloniki and in the midst of a group of University of Minnesota students visiting Greece, Laourdas and I engaged in a friendly debate about Kazantzakis and his place in modern Greek letters. Despite his critical attitude, Laourdas ended that debate with the following remarks which deserve recording: "Still, undeniably, Kazantzakis is a great writer, and the fact that we talk so passionately about his work today attests to his greatness." Neither was the dialogue between Laourdas and Kazantzakis totally broken, as is generally assumed. Three years after Laourdas' essay on the *Odyssey*, Kazantzakis sent him a copy of his new play *Capodistrias* with the inscription, "To the wise, beloved fellow fighter and friend," an indication, it seems, that despite ideological and other disagreements the two men maintained a profound respect for each other.

currents, Kazantzakis could be the point of departure for a variety of researches in the Greek intellectual world."[8]

It is this convergence of movements and currents in the person and work of Nikos Kazantzakis that prompted me to suggest him as the lecture topic to be offered in connection with the dedication of the Basil Laourdas Modern Greek Collection. The relationship of Kazantzakis and Laourdas, needless to say, played a role. And the fact that the Laourdas Library contains a rich collection of Kazantzakiana, including a copy of the original edition of the *Odyssey* with Laourdas' marginalia, was further inducement. There were two other reasons: October 26, 1977, marked the twentieth anniversary of the death of Kazantzakis and this was an opportunity to honor him in some way; and Kimon Friar, the friend and translator of Kazantzakis, was in the United States.

Kimon Friar is largely responsible for the promotion of Nikos Kazantzakis to the English-speaking world. In fact, it is difficult to dissociate the two. It is difficult to dissociate Kimon Friar from the promotion of modern Greek studies in general and poetry in particular in the English-speaking world, especially the United States. He has translated most of the modern Greek poets into English.[9] But the pride of his translation accomplishments is, of course, the *Odyssey*, as the latter was the pride of Kazantzakis' accomplishments. It was a Herculean task and an unusual collaboration between Kazantzakis and Friar which led to a moving intimate friendship, and which is reflected in the letters from Kazantzakis to Friar printed in this volume. Kazantzakis was fully appreciative of Friar's creative powers as a translator and of his devotion to the *Odyssey*. Gradually, he came to depend almost desperately on him as the man who would make available to the English-speaking world his *magnum opus*.

Friar did not disappoint him, even though, unfortunately, the *Odyssey* did not appear in English until a year after Kazantzakis' death. For four years Friar labored faithfully over the translation of the *Odyssey* getting to know both the author and the work intimately. The result was worth all the intellectual and physical investment. The *Odyssey* of Kazantzakis became *The Odyssey: A Modern Sequel* of Kimon Friar, one is tempted to say. It was a work of art in its own right and was received as such by the majority of the critics in the United States and England as the sample of reviews at the end of this volume remind us.

---

[8] C. Th. Dimaras, *op. cit.*, p. 455.
[9] See especially the anthology *Modern Greek Poetry*, translation, introduction, an essay on translation and notes by Kimon Friar (New York: Simon and Schuster, 1973).

Rarely has an epic of this size enjoyed the popularity, commercial success and critical appraise which befell the *Odyssey*. It is after all, intellectually, an extremely demanding work. Yet it is read by scholars, students and by business executives. The interest in the work may be partly the result of Kazantzakis' ability to capture in the person and struggle of the modern Odysseus at least some of the existential concerns of twentieth-century man. In the final analysis, the *Odyssey* may have succeeded partly because of the way Friar has cared for it even after its publication in English. For even though he resides in Greece, he returns to the United States either as a visiting professor or as a lecturer on topics of modern Greek literature and culture. He has lectured to hundreds of universities and institutions in the United States, South America and Greece. He is tireless even when he speaks to individuals about his work or about modern Greek writers. He became especially known for his lecture on Kazantzakis' *The Odyssey: A Modern Sequel* and *The Saviors of God,* which he gave repeatedly after the publication of his translation in 1958. His lecture on the *Odyssey* had acquired the reputation of a classic.

When I invited Kimon Friar to deliver his lecture on "The Spiritual Odyssey of Nikos Kazantzakis" on the occasion of the dedication of the Basil Laourdas Library, I expressed interest in having his talk published. He informed me that he had often been asked for copies of his talk but that he had always demurred, although he had generously permitted tapes to be made of it for student and broadcast use. His reluctance stemmed from several reasons: because he wished to continue giving it as a talk unavailable in printed form, because much of what he recounts here can be found in other forms in various of his publications on Kazantzakis, but primarily because he felt that the style of a talk differs from the style of the written word, being much simpler, less subordinated, so shaped as to create an impact and to be understood on first hearing. Much of the effectiveness of his talk depended, he believed, almost as much on its delivery as on what it had to say. Nevertheless, because requests for this talk have increased over the years, and because he no longer feels impelled to give it often, he has kindly consented to its publication, though with some trepidation, hoping that it might revive pleasant memories in those of his readers who have heard him deliver it or to introduce a masterpiece to those who knew little of Kazantzakis. With some minor additions, "The Spiritual Odyssey of Nikos Kazantzakis" is substantially the same talk Friar gave in the Special Collections section of the O. Meredith Wilson Library at the University of Minnesota for the inauguration of the Basil Laourdas Modern Greek Collection on May 19, 1978. The publication of this talk has been enriched by some letters Kazantzakis wrote to Friar during their collaboration, some reviews of *The Odyssey: A Modern Sequel* soon after its initial publication in 1958, by a photograph of the two poets during the time of their collaboration, and by Salvador Dali's "Homage to Homer: The Return of Ulysses." By way of contrast, Dali's work, depicting the rejoicing of the Gods over the return of the Homeric Odysseus, heightens the decision of Kazantzakis' hero, the modern Odysseus, to leave Ithaca again, in defiance of Gods and mortals.

It is a minor detail to be sure, but a pleasant one that Kimon Friar was in Minnesota at the University of Minnesota in Duluth when he was first approached by Simon and Schuster to undertake his translation of the *Odyssey*, and that his talk, on the same subject, was delivered at the University of Minnesota in Minneapolis in connection with the celebration of May 19, 1978. In a way, then, the present volume is a tribute to Nikos Kazantzakis and Kimon Friar the poets as well as to Basil Laourdas the neohellenist.

Theofanis G. Stavrou
University of Minnesota
May 18, 1979

THE SPIRITUAL ODYSSEY OF NIKOS KAZANTZAKIS

I was teaching at the Duluth branch of the University of Minnesota in 1954 when I received a telegram from Max Schuster of Simon and Schuster asking if I would undertake the translation of Nikos Kazantzakis' epical poem, the *Odyssey*. He had gone to Antibes on the French Riviera, where Kazantzakis was then living, to sign him up for more novels after the great success his firm had in publishing *Zorba the Greek*. In Athens, previously, his wife, Ray, had bought one of the rare copies of the first de luxe edition of the poem, 10 by 15 inches, 835 pages, published in 1938 in a limited edition of 301 copies. On Kazantzakis' desk now he saw another such copy. "What exactly is this monster?" he asked. "Read me some of it." As Kazantzakis read in his sonorous Greek, with gestures and intonations appropriate to that epic, Schuster's eyes lit up, and although he had not understood a single word, he cried out, "This is a book I must publish!," for since childhood he had been inordinately fond of Homer's own *Odyssey*. Obviously, he had forgotten, or was unaware, that I had submitted such a proposal to his publishing house (and to fifteen other firms) a few years previously, and had been refused. "But who can possibly translate such a monstrous work?" he inquired, and to my eternal pride Kazantzakis answered, "Only one man in the world." "And where is he?" Schuster asked. "In a place called Duluth," Kazantzakis answered.

And so it was I received that fateful telegram in Duluth from Schuster and Kazantzakis in Antibes. I replied immediately how much I had always wanted to translate that masterpiece, but my duties at the university would permit me to work only in the summers, and to translate only into prose, for if I attempted a metrical translation and kept my university position, the work might take me a dozen years or more.

I had first met Kazantzakis in a student's hostel in Florence in the summer of 1951 on my way to the United States. We had spoken together barely a half hour when he asked me suddenly if I had read all his work, for I gave him the impression that I understood his thought better than any man he knew, with the exception of Pandelis Prevelakis, his friend of some forty years. No, I answered; I had only read the forty very small sections Nikos Hadjikyriakos-Ghika had chosen to illustrate with ink drawings, together with the synopsis Kazantzakis had written to bind them into one unity. This is what I had translated into prose, had submitted to various publishing firms, and had been rejected.

When in June of 1954 I sailed to Antibes and collaborated with Kazantzakis for four months, we verified that we did indeed have an astonishing rapport between us. He could anticipate my every thought, and I his. Between us a deep relationship blossomed, as between son and spiritual father. We would sit side by side at his desk, and as he read from the Greek text, I would ask him questions, and thus filled several notebooks with exegesis on difficult words, phrases, images, meanings, nuances, or whatever else might help me toward an accurate translation.

While still in Antibes, I translated the entire sixth book into prose, but I was not satisfied. Kazantzakis' rich imagery and metaphors would sink in the shallow waters of prose rhythms; they seemed to need the buoyancy and weight of deep rhythmical waters to keep them afloat on meters of wave length. Therefore I tried translating various sections in a variety of meters, in pentameter, hexameter, heptameter, and in the original feminine iambic octameter. Some of these experiments, together with translations into prose, I sent to various friends and acquaintances: to T. S. Eliot, Archibald MacLeish, Allen Tate, Conrad Aiken, Theodore Weiss, James Laughlin, Tennessee Williams, Arthur Miller, Gore Vidal, and to several others. All replied that I must translate this great work into meter.

This placed me in a considerable dilemma. It would be impossible to translate into meter and to retain my position at the university. Unable to obtain a leave of absence, I resigned, therefore, accepted a very small stipend from Simon and Schuster, together with a Fulbright grant as Research Scholar at the University of Athens, and in October of 1954 left Antibes for Greece to begin an Odyssey of my own. I traveled through most of Greece on a motorscooter I had bought in Naples, translating as I went, and wandering through many of the Aegean islands, living in third-rate whitewashed inns, often working in island taverns or on small iron tables by the seaside, nibbling on the tentacles of octopi and sipping that notorious Greek wine, retsina, which to the uninitiated tastes like turpentine. Every time I completed one book of the twenty-four, I would send a copy to Kazantzakis in Antibes, with many questions, and he would answer me immediately with detailed replies. When I had half finished the epic in this manner, he and I met again, alone, in adjoining rooms, in the old Austrian-Hungarian Alps near Bled in Yugoslavia, and went over the entire twelve books I had translated. After that, I continued my peregrinations, and when I had finished the entire twenty-four books, we met, for the last time, in Antibes again, in May of 1957, and went over my entire translation. Then I left for my parents' home in a suburb of Chicago, where I put the finishing touches to my translation, gave it to my publishers, and left for a ten-month tour throughout South America as galley and page proofs followed me frantically to Antofagasta, Santiago, Puerto Montt, Aisén, Coyhaique, Buenos Aires, Montevideo, San Paulo, and Rio de Janeiro where I finally collapsed on the beach at Copacabana.

Last October marked the twentieth year of Kazantzakis' death. Twenty years ago when I had been in Antibes saying goodbye, he had suddenly burst into tears, and when I asked his wife why, she replied he had a premonition that we would never meet again. Twenty years previously, forty years ago, he had gone to China under the old regime, and now he was on his way there again, insatiably eager to see and understand what new culture and civilization were taking root there. The last communication I had from him was a postcard from Peking of a bird perched on a blossoming cherry bough. He wrote me: "We bring you into our minds, into our hearts every moment. I force my body to obey my soul, and thus I never tire. I am saying farewell to all things, and all things are saying farewell to me. Nevermore! The fairy tale is coming to an end." These were his last words to me. His premonition was coming true.

Nikos Kazantzakis was born in Iraklion, Crete, in 1883, and he died in Freiburg, Germany, in 1957. He is the author of about thirteen novels, for which he is best known; of about twenty dramas, most of them in poetic form; of three philosophical studies, one on Nietzsche, one on Bergson, and one on his own vision of life, about which I shall speak to you later. He has written travel books on Spain, Greece, England, China, Japan, Israel, Russia, hundreds of articles for newspapers and encyclopedias, and dozens of books for the public schools of Greece. In addition, he has translated into modern Greek all of Homer's *Iliad* and *Odyssey*, all of Dante's *Divine Comedy*, the first part of Goethe's *Faust*, Nietzsche's *The Birth of Tragedy*, Bergson's *On Laughter*, Darwin's *The Origin of Species*, and about forty other books. Furthermore, he has written two books of poetry. The first, entitled *Terza Rima*, written in Dante's stanza form, is composed of separate poems about the men and women who have influenced him most in life: poems, that is, on Dante, Shakespeare, St. Teresa, Moses, Mohammed, El Greco, Lenin, Don Quixote, Ghenghis Khan, his ancestors, his wife, himself. And then, of course, he has dared to write a sequel to Homer's *Odyssey*, but three times the size of that original epic, in 33,333 lines of feminine iambic octameter, and which I have translated into 33,333 lines of iambic hexameter of variable masculine and feminine endings. When he entitled his poem simply *Odyssey*, I imagine he hoped that when future generations were discussing a poem called *Odyssey*, someone would ask "Whose poem do you mean?" It is I who have added the subtitle *A Modern Sequel*.

Kazantzakis begins his epic with a Prologue to the Sun, for the entire poem is sunwashed and sundrenched in the brilliant light of Greece. The Sun itself is a personification in the poem; it talks, walks, and weeps with him on his adventures. And here in the Prologue, one of the main themes is stated: the theme that all matter, all water, stone, fire and earth must, eventually, in the evolution of nature, be transformed into spirit. Here is the passage:

> O Sun, my quick coquetting eye, my redhaired hound,
> sniff out all quarries that I love, give them swift chase,
> tell me all that you've seen on earth, all that you've heard,
> and I shall pass them through my entrail's secret forge,
> till slowly, with profound caresses, play, and laughter,
> stones, water, fire, and earth shall be transformed to spirit,
> and the mud-winged and heavy soul, freed of its flesh,
> shall like a flame serene ascend and fade in the sun.

And the Prologue ends:

> Ahoy, cast wretched sorrow out, prick up your ears —
> I sing the sufferings and the torments of renowned Odysseus.

Book I then begins, in a violent and aggressive manner. I know of no other epic poem that begins so ferociously. You will remember that toward the end of Homer's *Odyssey*, Odysseus has killed the suitors of his wife, Penelope, and that his body becomes drenched with blood. Kazantzakis has grafted his poem on this section of Homer's epic in Book XXII. It begins with an "And," as though it were directly continuing the previous poem. Here is the opening:

> And when in his wide courtyards Odysseus had cut down
> the insolent youths, he hung on high his sated bow
> and strode to the warm bath to cleanse his bloodstained body.

Two slaves prepared his bath, but when they saw their lord they shrieked with terror, for his loins and belly steamed, and thick black blood dripped down from both his murderous palms.

Kazantzakis used to say to me, pounding his table in rhythm to the meter, tasting and emphasizing each syllable, "And thick black blood dripped down! Ah, if only I had monosyllables!" The Greek language, like all inflected languages, is highly polysyllabic and has practically no monosyllables. I am sure you would like to hear this passage in Kazantzakis' own demotic Greek:

Σὰν πιὰ ποθέρισε τοὺς γαύρους νιοὺς μὲς στὶς φαρδιὲς αὐλές του,
τὸ καταχόρταστο ἀνακρέμασε δοξάρι του ὁ Δυσσέας
καὶ διάβη στὸ θερμὸ λουτρό, τὸ μέγα του κορμὶ νὰ πλύνει.
Δυὸ δοῦλες συγκερνοῦσαν τὸ νερό, μὰ ὡς εἶδαν τὸν ἀφέντη
μπῆξαν φωνή, γιατὶ ἡ σγουρὴ κοιλιὰ καὶ τὰ μεριά του ἀχνίζαν
καὶ μαῦρα στάζαν αἵματα πηχτὰ κι ἀπὸ τὶς δυό του φοῦχτες.

During a festival held in Ithaca one day, a minstrel sings of how three godfathers had blessed the infant Odysseus in his cradle. The first godfather was Tantalus, who was punished by never being able to drink the receding water toward which he stooped, nor grasp the fruit he tried to reach. He was being, as we say today, "tantalized," and it was he who bequeathed to Odysseus the never-satisfied, the ever-hungry heart. The second godfather was Heracles, who had performed the twelve Herculean labors, and who bequeathed to Odysseus the *thirteenth* labor, still to be performed. The third godfather was Prometheus, the hero who had stolen fire from the tyrant, Zeus, and had given it to mankind. He bequeathed to Odysseus the humanistic heart, ever rebellious against tyranny and oppression.

But Odysseus becomes bored with his island home of Ithaca, for which he had longed almost twenty years. He becomes bored with his timid and pragmatic son, Telemachus; and he becomes infinitely bored with his good and patient wife, Penelope. He resolves, therefore, to leave all this far behind, to sail off on further adventures, to explore new horizons. He gathers together a motley crew. There is Captain Clam, an old sea-wolf; there is Orpheus, a scraggly and timid poetaster; there is Hardihood, a brawny coppersmith; there is Granite, a stalwart young man of the mountains; and above all there is Kentaur, a mountain of meat, whom he found drunk in a gutter, and to whom he said: "Come along as ballast for my ship! And besides, such a mountain of meat can be transformed into much spirit."

They build a skiff and set sail for Sparta, for it's Odysseus' intention to visit his old friend of the Trojan Wars, King

Menelaus, and to induce him to come along on further adventures. They land in the Peloponnesus, and as Odysseus and Kentaur make their way toward the palace, they see on the road a horde of Dorian barbarians who have been inundating the country from the North. These represent for Kazantzakis the new, savage, barbarous blood that always descends on decaying, decadent civilizations and infuses them with new blood, much like the Huns, the Goths, and the Vandals, much, Kazantzakis thought, like the Russians today. When Odysseus reaches Sparta, he finds the peasants in revolt against their grasping King, but by threatening them with the possibility of a Doric attack unless they seek protection under their King's aegis, Odysseus persuades them to submit and obey. This trickery reveals Odysseus' aristocratic bias, but which, as we shall see, undergoes radical change as the poem progresses. When he tries to induce Menelaus to join him in further voyages, Menelaus refuses, for he is fat, content, and rich with the exploitation of his people. And besides, he has for wife again the most beautiful woman in the world. But Helen has become bored with her sedentary life in Sparta, and longs once more to become the adored of many men. And so, in a brilliant idea of Kazantzakis', the second willing abduction of Helen occurs.

Odysseus takes with him a brave young mountain shepherd, Rocky, and together with Helen and all his crew, they set sail again, but this time toward no certain destination. As they sail, a violent storm threatens to capsize their ship. Orpheus whines that God is demanding a sacrifice in expiation for the abduction of Helen, but though Hardihood approaches her to cast her into the waves, he finds that he cannot, overwhelmed by her beauty. Odysseus rejoices in his manliness and vows to make him King of the first land they sight. The storm subsides, they sight the island of Crete, and sail into the bustling harbor town of Knossos. Another old crony of Odysseus is on the throne, King Idomeneus, and Odysseus thinks he will be received with open arms. But Idomeneus has eyes only for Helen, and wishes to make her his bride in the orgiastic bull rituals that are to be held in the arena. Odysseus becomes so nauseated with the decadence of Knossos that he joins with Idomeneus' youngest daughter, Phida, and the slaves of the palace, in a revolt against her father. In the slaughter, Phida beheads her father, Knossos is burned to the ground, Odysseus makes Hardihood King, as he had promised, then marries Helen off to a young blond Dorian. This marriage symbolizes for Kazantzakis the mingling of Helen's old Achaean blood with the new blood that is to result in the Golden Age of Perikles.

During the turmoils in Knossos, Odysseus lies down by the riverbank and listens to a slave singing of freedom. Finally, as he drowses and falls asleep, his old companion, Death, makes the first of his many appearances, lies beside him in comradely embrace, and the two sleep together:

> Death came and stretched full length along the archer's side;
> weary from wandering all night long, his lids were heavy,
> and he, too, longed to sit and sleep awhile beside
> his old friend near the river, by a willow's shade.
> Throwing his bony arms across the archer's chest,
> he and his boon companion slowly sank in sleep.
> Death slept, and dreamt that man indeed, perhaps, existed,
> that houses rose on earth, perhaps, kingdoms and castles,
> that even gardens rose and that beneath their shade
> court ladies strolled in languor and handmaidens sang.
> He dreamt there was a sun that rose, a moon that shone,
> a wheel of earth that turned and very season brought,
> perhaps, all kinds of fruit and flowers, cooling rain and snow,
> and that it turned once more, perhaps, till earth renewed.
> But Death smiled secretly in sleep for he knew well
> this was but dream, a dappled wind, toy of his weary mind,
> and unperturbed, allowed this evil dream to goad him.
> But slowly life took courage, and the wheel whirled round,
> earth gaped with hunger, sun and rain sank in her bowels,
> unnumbered eggs hatched birds, the world was filled with worms,
> until a packed battalion of beasts, men and thoughts
> set out and pounced on sleeping Death to eat him whole.
> A human pair crouched in his nostrils' heaving caves,
> there lit and fed a fire, set up their house and cooked,
> and from Death's upper lip hung down their new son's cradle.
> Feeling his nostrils tingling and his pale lips tickled,
> Death suddenly shook and tossed in sleep, and the dream vanished.
> For a brief moment Death had fallen asleep and dreamt of life.

Restless once more, Odysseus sets out on further adventures. He is now impelled by that old dream of ancient explorers: that of finding the source of the Nile. He sets off for Egypt, therefore, and as he sails up the Nile, he sees misery and poverty everywhere. Here the gods are still half man and half beast, and not like the Olympian gods, half man and half god. Although Odysseus had long ago abandoned the twelve Olympian gods, he is still a man in search of his soul, of a new god.

In Egypt he conducts what must be among the first archeological digs in literature, and in the tomb of an ancient king finds a treasure of gold and precious jewels. He and his crew load down their ship almost to sinking with all this treasure, but as they sail he discovers that not only his crew, but that also he himself is now thinking of settling down, of building estates and villas on the Nile, of leading the good, comfortable, bourgeoise life. He commands, therefore, that all this treasure, even the smallest gold coin, be cast overboard, and he exclaims:

> If I could choose what gods to carry on all my ships,
> I'd choose both War and Hunger, that fierce and fruitful pair.

For Odysseus knows well that new horizons are never gained by satisfied and comfortable men, but by those who are always at war — with themselves; who are always hungry — to explore new regions of thought.

This impetuous and grand gesture of casting treasure into the river, I discovered later, was very characteristic of the man Kazantzakis himself. When he was a young man of about thirty or so, he went to Assisi to study the life of his favorite saint, St. Francis. He lived in the house of the Contessa Enrichetta, an old aristocrat then in her eighties. She would be waiting for him every evening by the fireside with a cup of tea, and as they drank and conversed, a deep and endearing love blossomed between the old Contessa and the young man. When he was about to leave, she begged him to remain, offering to make him her heir, to leave him all her possessions; but he replied sadly that he had many new horizons to explore, and could not remain. However, he made a date with her for lunch, to be kept ten years later. Ten years later, he was in Spain reporting on the Civil War. Suddenly, he remembered his date with the Contessa, and what I admire most is that he never troubled to find out if the Contessa, now in her nineties, was still alive. He took a plane immediately to Assisi, bought flowers and fruit, and knocked on her door. It was opened by her maid who said, without an iota of surprise, "Mr. Kazantzakis, the Contessa is expecting you. You will lunch together in her boudoir, for she is rather old and slightly indisposed." He found her propped up on her pillows, dressed in her finest laces, and they fell weeping into each other's arms. After he had presented her with the flowers and fruit, they lunched together, talking of old time and of their affection. Then Kazantzakis returned to Spain, and the old Contessa, of course, died soon after, having stubbornly sustained her life for this rendezvous. People capable of making such grand and impetuous gestures are my kind of people.

Soon after casting treasure into the river, Odysseus joins a young communist leader, the Jewish girl, Rala, in a revolution against the Pharaoh and his decadent priests, in direct contrast to his opposition of the Spartan peasants before the palace of Menelaus. But the army of the Pharaoh defeats the army of the workers, and Rala and Odysseus are thrown into a dungeon. There he has many horrible nightmares of a new god whose face and body are tortured and tormented; but whenever he tries to carve out this face into a mask, he discovers that he is always carving out his own tortured and tormented face. One day, by royal command, he slings such a mask over his shoulders and dances, a la Zorba, before the Pharaoh. Suddenly, in the climax of the dance, he claps the mask over his face, and the Pharaoh is so terrified of this vision of a new and tormented god that he drives Odysseus out of Egypt, fearful even of having him assassinated.

Odysseus now gathers a rough-and-tumble crew of thieves, adventurers, gamblers and beggars, the persecuted and the driven, the kind of people who have no hope of a better life where they are and who long for a new, virgin land in which to settle. Odysseus, as you see, has been slowly evolving from an adventurous and pagan hero into a kind of Hebraic figure, much like Moses, leading his children out of Egypt and toward the Promised Land.

After many tribulations, they do discover the lake source of the Nile, situated at the foot of a tall mountain. Odysseus sets his men to building what he hopes will be a new and ideal city, far from the contaminations of the *then* modern civilizations; but we know this to be a vain dream, a dream that impelled Plato in his *Republic*, St. Augustine in his *City of God*, Sir Thomas Moore in his *Utopia*.

Odysseus, meanwhile, ascends to the very top of the mountain, and there, like Moses, communes with his god for seven days and seven nights. Then he descends from the mountain, bringing his people new commandments by which to live, on which to establish a new civilization. This is embodied in Books XIV and XVI of the *Odyssey*, but it is given its fullest treatment in another book by Kazantzakis which I have translated, *The Saviors of God: Spiritual Exercises*. Here, in a passionate and poetic style, Kazantzakis has set down the core of his vision of life. It is the key to all his work, and he has tried to give it varied form in the novel, the drama, the travelogue, in journalism, in epic poetry, and even in political action. Toward the end of this talk, I shall tell you what vision it was that Odysseus saw on the top of the mountain, and what new commandments he received from his new god.

Odysseus now descends from the mountain with these new commandments, and for a year he and his troops busy themselves with building their new Utopia, their Ideal City, their Land of the

Heart's Desire. But on the very day when they are inaugurating and celebrating their new city, the earth begins to tremble, the mountain begins to erupt with fire and lava, the ground gapes wide, and the entire city and almost all of its inhabitants are swallowed up. This is a theme that occurs again and again in the *Odyssey* and in all of Kazantzakis' works: the theme that Nature, or God, is utterly indifferent to man's fate; that earthquakes, eruptions, floods, catastrophes, or wars wipe out all of man's endeavors; that man is always building for the sheer joy of building, of creating, and not for any hope or reward, knowing full well that he is but the smallest link in the evolution of Nature, or God.

As he sits now at the edge of the abyss where all his hopes and his dreams have been swallowed up, Odysseus' hair turns white with agony. He rages against a god who has made the world so imperfect that man is forced into an attempt to perfect it himself. His mind marches on beyond all sorrow or joy or hope. He falls now into the "terror of thought," into an inner contemplation that blazes with light. He identifies himself now with all of Nature, with snakes and the grass, with the ruthless laws of death and destruction, with insects and fruits and flowers, with all animate and inanimate things. His feet flow like a river; morning glories twine themselves about his body; nightingales perch on his head and burst into song; fireflies come and glow in his beard all night long; and he comes to a tragic acceptance of life as it is, but he accepts this with joy, and blesses each of his five senses. He blesses his restless search: "My soul," he cries out, "your voyages have been your native land!"

Now Death becomes his constant companion. Stooping with humility, he kisses Mother Earth and accepts the entire universe, both good and evil. He has now become a famous ascetic throughout Africa, and as he begins his long trek through the heart of that dark continent toward its most southern tip, he meets on the way various representatives of various ways of life.

One day he sees approaching the caravan of a mighty Prince, the type of Buddha. This young man had once seen fearful signs of man's decay. He had seen a beautiful young man dead in the prime of life. He had seen disease ravaging the body of an old man; and now he roams the world in anguish, seeking to find the answers to evil, to decay, to death. When the Prince wants to know what happens to the body when a man dies, his slave tries to dissuade him from finding out, but when the Prince insists, the slave answers that the corpse is eaten up by six waves of worms, and the Prince weeps, unable to accept such horror. He begs Odysseus to give him some hope that he might not see the face of death in all things, but Odysseus replies that he and the Prince have looked beyond the gods, beyond hope, and into the face of death, but whereas the Prince sinks nerveless to the ground, "I," says Odysseus, "I hold death like a black banner, and march on." Then in one of the strongest lines in the *Odyssey*, Odysseus says: "Death is the salt that gives to life its tasty sting!" Without the constant presence of death we should never know the value and beauty of life.

Soon afterward, Odysseus meets the famous courtesan, Margaro. He tells her that there are seven secret paths to salvation: through the mind, the heart, silence, activity, despair, war, and love, and that she has chosen the last, that which strives to merge opposites, male and female. And what is the love act in itself but the two dualities, male and female, trying to become one in actual bodily penetration as well as in soul, that which in ecstasy tries to break down the barriers of flesh? When Odysseus asks Margaro for the distillation of all her experience, she replies that she tells her lovers: "In all this wretched world, only you and I exist." And again: "Beloved, I feel at length that you and I are One." But Odysseus sadly replies that there is a third synthesis: "Even this One, O Margaro, even this One is empty air." Odysseus rejects Buddha's nihilism and Margaro's affirmation. Buddha cannot lift himself above the grave and Margaro cannot soar above the flesh. Odysseus affirms the tragic joy of life.

And now he comes to an ascetic who all his life long has pursued the eternal questions: Why were we born? For what purpose? Toward what goal? But now that he is dying, he regrets his ascetic and abstemious life, his search for God, and he wishes, instead, that he had lived like a mighty king, or like a great lover, or like a powerful conqueror. When he dies, his hand stretches out avidly for more, unsatisfied; and when the villagers come to bury him, they find they cannot make the hand bend or the palm close. Odysseus tells them that the hand will not close until they have filled it with their dearest treasure. Each interprets according to his idea of what constitutes treasure. The elders cast gold into the thirsty palm, but it will not close. The chieftains cast the bronze keys of their city, the young men their gleaming weapons, but the hand will not close. Mothers pour in their tears, maidens their kisses, and a child comes and on the little finger of the grasping hand hangs its only toy. But the hand will not close, and you begin to wonder: what will Odysseus, what will Kazantzakis find that will make the hand close? Odysseus stoops, gathers up a bit of earth, places it in the avid palm, and it closes, satisfied at last: "Dust thou art, and to dust thou shalt return."

He meets a Tragic King who tries to escape from the confines of his narrow kingdom, but who finds out that his realm is an island, and beyond its boundaries always roars the vast, infinite sea of annihilation. He realizes that man is forever caught in the round, cyclical trap of his own existence, of his given mind, his given limitations.

He meets Prince Elias who, despairing of ever becoming King, longs to be immortalized as a singer, a poet, but when he strikes up his lyre, all of its seven strings remain silent. He learns that in order for the lyre to sing it must be steeped in the blood of his seven sons. One by one he leads his sons to battle, and one by one he drenches each of the seven strings in his sons' blood. Now when he strikes the lyre, it bursts out into ecstatic song. Odysseus discovers that only through tragedy can man rise to song.

He meets Captain Sole, the type of Don Quixote, who has straddled his decrepit camel, Lightning, taken up his rusted sword and armor, and has sallied out to save the world from slavery and injustice. He has been captured by cannibals, bound to a stake by the very slaves he sought to free and is now being prepared for dinner. Odysseus saves this intrepid soul, but as soon as Captain Sole is released, he dashes once more to save the slaves, who will again bind him to a stake to prepare him for dinner. Odysseus admires this rash and rebellious heart, this imagination that dares to go beyond the possible, and yet he spurns it, for it dwells far from reality and practicality in a land of wish-fulfillment and fantasy only. He wishes Captain Sole well, and plods on, meeting other representative types.

He meets the Lord of the Tower, a hedonist who believes that best of all is the unconcerned, the uncommitted mind that flits from flower to flower, sucking up the sweets of existence, but never becomes involved in life itself. Odysseus spurns this man as the last dregs of a decadent existence.

He encounters an old Negro chieftain who is pursued and slain in a dark forest by his twelve sons, and who eat up their father bit by bit. Each son eats that portion of his father which contains the strength he would himself desire to possess: the eye for keen sight, the ear for sensitive hearing, the hand for brawny strength. You must not be horrified by this, for this is what we all do when we go to communion, but in a more civilized form, when we eat the wafer and drink the wine, the body and blood of Christ, in order to obtain the strength of the Savior. As Odysseus watches, he feels that he, too, in distant ages long past, had once killed his own father.

Finally, after months of trekking, he comes to the ocean on the southernmost tip of Africa, and as he proceeds at night to a bustling harbor town, he watches a strange and religious procession. He is told that some Cretans, who have been shipwrecked and have settled here, are now celebrating their new God. Some call him the Slayer, some call him the Savior, some call him the Messiah, but, he is told, the priests in their secret rituals call him — Odysseus! In ironic mockery, Odysseus exclaims:

> I've been reduced to a god that walks the earth like myth!
> O wretched soul of man, you can't stand free on earth
> or walk upright, unless you walk with fear or hope.
> When will companion souls like mine come down to earth!

One day Odysseus watches some black fishermen hauling in their catch, and among them he hears a young fisher lad speaking of one eternal Father who is Love, of the earth as a path that leads to Heaven. Another fisherman replies that all this is nonsense, unrealistic; that injustice rules the world rather, and not love; that evil thrives. But the fisher boy softly answers that if someone were to strike him on one cheek, he would turn the other. Odysseus says to himself that even this puny boy will defend himself if I strike him. He then hits the boy hard on one cheek, but to his amazement the boy does indeed meekly turn the other cheek. Odysseus is terrified at this new, revolutionary idea in the world: the idea that you may return good for evil, love for hate. The two sit down together by the edge of the sea, Odysseus and the black Jesus Christ, and converse all night long. Odysseus upholds the path of war and strife, the negro lad of love and peace, of an ultimate realm where man and God merge into One. Odysseus replies that even this One is empty air, but the negro lad insists that only this final One is real. Odysseus accuses the boy of loving only the soul of man, whereas he loves the flesh of man also, his stench, the earth, even death. Odysseus denies that the soul has any value apart from the flesh, for it must evolve in and through the flesh. They part affectionately at dawn.

In the meantime, Odysseus has built his last boat, a kind of Eskimo kayak. When he finishes it, he sees that it resembles a coffin. He realizes that he will now embark on his last voyage, and he exclaims that he has measured his own body, his heart and mind, the earth and sky, fear and love, the greatest happiness, the greatest pain, and that all his measurements have come to this: the coffin. He now sets sail toward the South Pole, and for a while lives among primitive people in a land of ice. Their gods are once again the primordial gods of Hunger and Fear and Cold. When he asks an old chieftain that highly sophisticated question, "What do you want out of life?," the old man gapes in astonishment at such a stupid question, and replies: "To eat!"

When the spring thaw comes, Odysseus bids these people farewell, and paddles away in his kayak. But as he waves from a distance, he sees that the ice splits open, gapes wide, and he watches in horror as all his friends and all their possessions are plunged into an icy abyss, exactly as his own Ideal City had been so ruthlessly swallowed up. Kazantzakis never permits us to forget the gaping annihilation that awaits us all, individually or together.

Finally Death comes, in person, and sits on the prow of Odysseus' little skiff. Odysseus welcomes him like an old and faithful friend, for who, or rather, what is Death? Death is your own body, your own flesh, you yourselves, for as the first century philosopher, Manilius, once informed us, we begin a parallel journey in life together with Death from the moment we have been conceived in our mother's womb. Wherever Odysseus has some mark on his body, Death has an identical mark on his own twin body. Death is our mirror image. As the two old cronies converse, Death turns into a Black Swan, into Dante's White Rose, and behind the White Rose there looms a huge iceberg, Odysseus' last ship of death. His kayak crashes on the iceberg; he clings to it with blooded fingernails and toenails; the cold South Wind strips him bare, and he now realizes that this is the moment of his death. He cries out to all those with whom in life he has lived through some intense relationship, friend or foe. They hear him and come running from all the ends of the earth to keep him company on his last voyage. If they have died, like Kentaur, they rise out of their graves, gathering up their moldering flesh, wiping away the worms from their eyelids. All run to bring him comfort. Some fly through the air, others speed over the water: Buddha and Margaro, Rala and Christ, Kentaur and Orpheus, Hardihood and Rocky, Helen and Diktena. From his island home of Ithaca, neither his wife Penelope, nor his son Telemachus hear his cry, but only his dog, Argos, who leaps out of his grave and runs, barking, to meet his master.

And finally his three godfathers come, Tantalus, and Heracles, and Prometheus, and stand like three tall masts on his ice ship of death. For this last moment of death Kazantzakis has found one of his most beautiful images. You have all seen a flame leap from its wick, leap from its body, the candle, and for a brief moment hang suspended in the air before it vanishes forever. In this eternal moment of the suspended candle flame, the entire twenty-fourth book of the *Odyssey* takes place in a kind of wild, Wagnerian operatic scene. Here is the image:

> As a low lantern's flame flicks in its final blaze
> then leaps above its shriveled wick and mounts aloft
> brimming with light, and soars toward Death with dazzling joy,
> so did his fierce soul leap before it vanished in air.

Odysseus' companions now hang on the three tall masts the pomegranates and the grapes and the figs of Greece, and as Odysseus plunges his face and body in the fruit, he dies. Here is the passage:

> Erect by his mid-mast amid the clustered grapes,
> the prodigal son now heard the song of all return,
> and his eyes cleansed and emptied, his full heart grew light,
> for Life and Death were songs, his mind the singing bird.
> He cast his eyes about him, slowly clenched his teeth,
> then thrust his hands in pomegranates, figs, and grapes
> until the twelve gods round his dark loins were refreshed.
> All the great body of the world-roamer turned to mist,
> and slowly his snowship, his memory, fruit and friends,
> drifted like fog far down the sea, vanished like dew.
> Then flesh dissolved, glances congealed, the heart's pulse stopped,
> and the great mind leaped to the peak of its holy freedom,
> fluttered with empty wings, then upright through the air
> soared high and freed itself from its last cage, its freedom.
> All things like frail mist scattered, till but one brave cry
> for a brief moment hung the calm, benighted waters:
> "Forward, my lads, sail on, for Death's breeze blows in a fair wind!"

Earlier in this talk I said that later I would speak to you of the vision Odysseus saw on the mountain's peak and what were the new commandments he received there from his god. These are embodied in Books XIV and XVI of the *Odyssey* and more fully delineated in *The Saviors of God: Spiritual Exercises*. In these books Kazantzakis declares that a man has Three Duties. The First Duty of man is to follow the mind, for it is the mind that imposes order on disorder. It formulates the laws without which we cannot live as a community; it is the rational system of things, that which builds bridges and institutions, which sets up rational boundaries beyond which the mind itself dares not go. It is logic, shape, form, pattern geometry, law, and may remind us of Edna St. Vincent Millay's lovely line, "Euclid alone has looked on beauty bare."

But the Second Duty of man is to go beyond the mind and to follow the heart, for the heart admits of no boundaries. It yearns to smash all frontiers, to pierce beyond all phenomena. It wants to merge with something beyond mind and matter; it has one foot on the cliff and the other foot dangling over the abyss.

The Third Duty of man, however, is to go beyond the hope which the mind and heart seem to offer. Man must free himself from the hope that the mind can indeed impose order on disorder, that the heart can indeed find out the essence of things, and then he must fight on, without hope or salvation of any kind. He must say that nothing exists, neither life nor death, and he must accept this *necessity* bravely; indeed, with exultation and song. So far as I know, only the ancient Greeks had a goddess whom they named Necessity, *Anange*. Because Kazantzakis so strongly emphasizes the ultimate annihilation that awaits us all, many think of him as a desperado, as a nihilist; but he is not, for he insists that exactly on this annihilating abyss man must build the affirmative structure of his life. He must say the almighty "Yes!" over that other almighty "No!," and then he must build over this abyss in an ecstacy of tragic joy.

After these Three Duties, a man is then prepared to undertake a pilgrimage of Four Steps. At the start of his journey, he hears an agonized cry within him shouting for help. His First Step, therefore, is to plunge within himself, into his own Ego, into his own uniqueness, for we are all the products of a heritage and of an environment we never chose for ourselves. We never chose our parents or our country, nor the century into which we should have liked to have been born. We never chose the religious or the political credos we accept on faith since infancy. We become the products of certain glands, brain matter, environment; and yet, nevertheless, we feel that down deep beneath all these layers of given flesh, time, and place, something uniquely our own lies hidden. Perhaps in early adolescence, in our college years, we try to form our true selves, out of time and out of space, an ideal self. We feel that we are agonizingly unique. We pass before a mirror and we fail to recognize the reflection, for in our inner reflection we are something utterly different. We feel our bodies to be prisons composed of flesh, blood, veins, nerves — dungeons in which our true selves have been abandoned. Often my students come to me in despair, in humiliation, in utter self-abnegation, and I become furious with them. I tell them: "But each of you is utterly unique. Nothing like you has ever existed in the entire universe, and nothing like you shall ever exist again . . . You may be a horrible example of what is unique — but unique you are!"

Man's First Step, then, is to plunge deep down within himself until he discovers that what is crying out within himself for salvation is the very endangered spirit of God Himself — or what man has hitherto designated with that word "God." When I asked Kazantzakis why he so often used a word so worn and corroded with convention, he replied, most beautifully, I think, that it is the most wounded word in history and deserves this honor. In order to free this endangered spirit of God within himself, a man must consider himself to be solely responsible for the salvation of the world, for when a man dies, the unique play of his mind crashes into ruin forever.

In his Second Step, a man must plunge beyond his ego and into his racial origins. He must consider that he comes from one particular race, from one particular tradition in history; that he is also uniquely a Jew, or a Greek, or a Hindu, or a Black. He must search among his racial ancestors to find those spirits who may help him toward a greater refinement of spirit, toward more and more light. Like the Odysseus in Homer's *Odyssey*, he must descend into Hades in order to speak to the shades of his ancestral dead; but he must choose ruthlessly among them. He must, for instance, say "Yes" to Aristotle and "No" to Plato; "Yes" to Sappho" and "No" to Pindar; "Yes" to Aeschylus and "No" to Euripides — or vice versa. He must then pass on this knowledge to his children and encourage them to reach him and to surpass him.

In his Third Step a man must plunge beyond his ego, beyond his own particular race, and into the races of all mankind. He must acknowledge himself as belonging to the species *man*; that in his blood there is nothing pure; that through his veins flows the blood of Black, of Jew, of Greek, of Hindu, of Hottentot: the blood of all races from the most simple to the most complex; and then he must embrace the races of all mankind within himself in the struggle to liberate the spirit of God within himself that is shouting for help.

And now you wonder: what can Odysseus, what can Kazantzakis possibly find as the Fourth Step, that goes beyond mankind itself? But Kazantzakis insists, that just as a man must go beyond his mind and his heart, beyond hope, beyond his race and the races of all mankind, he must also plunge beyond mankind itself and become identified with all of matter, with the entire universe. He insists that there is no distinction between animate and inanimate matter, that man must therefore identify himself with earth and stone and sea, with plants, animals, insects, and birds, with the vital impulse of all creation in all phenomena. Each man is a fathomless, a bottomless composite of atavistic roots that plunge down deep into obscure and primordial origins. A man must now enter into a mystic communication with the entire universe. We have all felt like this to some degree or other, perhaps often when walking along the oceanside at midnight, when we hear the pounding of the surf beating in rhythm with the pounding of our hearts, or when we look up at the stars and remember George Meredith's immortal line describing the wheeling of the stars in their orbits: "That army of unutterable law." It is then we find that the wheeling of the stars in their orbits, the pounding of the sea, and the pounding of our hearts are all one rhythm, are all one universe. This is what Kazantzakis means, this mystical communication.

But for Kazantzakis it is *now* that man is prepared to go even further still, beyond the mind, the heart, beyond hope, beyond his ego, his race, the races of all mankind, beyond all phenomena, and plunge into what he calls a Vision of the Invisible walking on all things visible. The essence of this Invisible, according to Kazantzakis, is an agonized ascent toward more and more purity of spirit, toward more and more light. The goal is the very struggle itself, and this evolutionary ascent is endless.

In this conception, God is not a perfect and complete Being, there, somewhere out in timeless space; but God is a spiritual concept which is itself evolving toward purity as man himself evolves. If I am not mistaken, modern theologians have recently come to this position, unaware, I suppose, that poets have known about it for centuries.

In this conception, God is not All-Holy. He is pitiless. He chooses only the best, only those who are strong enough to survive. He does not care either for men or ideas or virtues. He exploits them all for a moment; He manipulates them in a never-ceasing, evolutionary struggle to create something finer, more spiritual, but in His agonized attempt He smashes them and tries to free Himself for further, more spiritual creations. Our earth since its inception has seen more than one hundred million species, and already ninety-eight per cent of these have irretrievably vanished in God's, or Nature's, constant turmoil of creative evolution.

In this conception, God is not All-Knowing. His head is a confused jumble of light and dark. He cries out to man to help Him, because man is, in the present stage of evolution, the holiest carrier of God. Man is God's highest spiritual reach thus far, in the present stage of man's and God's evolution. God cannot be saved unless man tries to save Him by struggling with Him; nor can man be saved unless God is saved. It is in this sense that man is the Savior of God. On the whole, according to Kazantzakis, it is man who must save God.

When a man has had this vision of the spirit that is always struggling, always evolving, always unsatisfied, shouting for help, he must then try to give it body in deed and in action, in art, institutions, science, law, even in political action, but he must realize that any such attempt necessarily pollutes the vision, that the thing realized is always — but *always* — a betrayal of the thing envisaged. And yet man must accept this imperfectability of his and must struggle with it in a never-ending and ever-ascending battle.

The entire theme of *The Saviors of God* and of the *Odyssey* is, as you have seen: What — not Who — but What is God? What is Freedom? The essence of God is the attempt to find freedom, to throw off all regional shackles that impede our onward progress in the universe. We must never be content with the dogmas and credos given us by the accident of our birth in a certain century, in a particular time and place on this earth, but we must try to break through the narrow confines of faith, whether in religion, in politics, in economics, whether the ties of home or country or tradition, and like an eagle view the world from as high a perspective as we can; and we must even beware lest the pursuit of freedom itself does not petrify into mechanical action. We must say to ourselves that no ultimate freedom, no ultimate salvation exists, and then we must accept this with heroic pessimism, with erotic stoicism, with tragic joy.

Kazantzakis is buried on top of one of the bastions which are part of the old Venetian wall surrounding the city of Iraklion in Crete where he was born. The tomb itself is hewn out of black Cretan marble, jagged, crude, cracked, and unpolished, surmounted by a tall, simple cross composed of two unplaned branches of a Cretan tree. And there you will find no name to designate who lies there, you will find no date of birth or death. You will only find this legend carved on bronze:

I do not hope for anything,
I do not fear anything,
I am free.

According to Kazantzakis, the forces that drive us on are not the forces of justice, of kindness, of plenty, of peace. The forces that drive us on are those of injustice, of cruelty, of hunger, of war. It is man's eternal glory and his nobility that it is *he* who has created the concepts of justice, of kindness, of plenty, of peace, and it is by this definition that he is the holiest carrier of God, is God's highest spiritual reach, thus far. Nature, or God, are indifferent to these concepts, for they are purely the creations of man himself — although, of course, man is himself one of the infinite products of Nature, or of God. God is never created out of happiness or comfort, but out of tragedy and strife. The greatest virtue is not to be free, but to struggle unceasingly for freedom.

Finally, Kazantzakis ends with an image, a symbol. The universe, he says, is a blossoming Tree of Fire. Fire is the first and the last mask of God, and at the very summit of this Tree of Fire there bursts into blossom a final fruit. The final fruit of flame, says Kazantzakis, is light. And one day the entire universe will vanish into the deepest and most distilled essence of the spirit where all contradictions shall at last be resolved, and this is the quintessence of silence. For as Hamlet says in dying, "The rest is silence."

Now I must inform you of a most strange, of a most mysterious coincidence. Odysseus is obviously Kazantzakis' autobiographical hero. All of his books are in some sense a personal confession. Kazantzakis has brought Odysseus to die near the South Pole, but when he was last in China he was given smallpox and typhoid injections in Canton on his way to Tokyo. Because he had been suffering from lymphoid leukemia during the past eight years, these injections poisoned his right arm. He kept this hidden from his wife, until in Tokyo it became too obvious to be hidden any longer. The wound was turning into gangrene. With death now in his veins, Kazantzakis was flown across the North Pole toward his ultimate death in a clinic in Freiburg.

Odysseus died near the South Pole, and Kazantzakis carried death in his veins over the North Pole. It is almost as though he willed such a death for himself, for between the two of them, thus, at the earth's two poles, at the earth's antipodes — or so I like to think — they held between themselves the entire world in a loving, a living, an intense embrace.

In the opening of the twenty-third book of the *Odyssey*, Kazantzakis has written an epitaph for his autobiographical hero that in truth best suits himself. I should like to see it engraved in marble and erected by the side of his solitary grave in Iraklion. It reads:

> Great Sun, flood down into his bowels, turn all the worms
> to thousands of huge crimson-golden butterflies!
> In a great blaze of wings and light, in salt embrace,

make Death come riding down astride a gallant thought!
Let Death come down to craven heads and slavish souls
with his sharp scythe and barren bones, but let him come
to this lone man like a great lord to knock with shame
on his five famous castle doors, and with great awe
plunder whatever dregs that in the ceaseless strife
of his staunch body he had not found time to turn
from flesh and bone into pure spirit, lightning, deeds, and joy.
The Archer has fooled you, Death, he has squandered all your goods,
melted down all the rusts and rots of his foul flesh
till they escaped you in pure spirit, and when you come
you'll find but trampled fires, embers, ash, and fleshly dross.

KIMON FRIAR

Salvador Dali: "Homage to Homer: The Return of Ulysses"

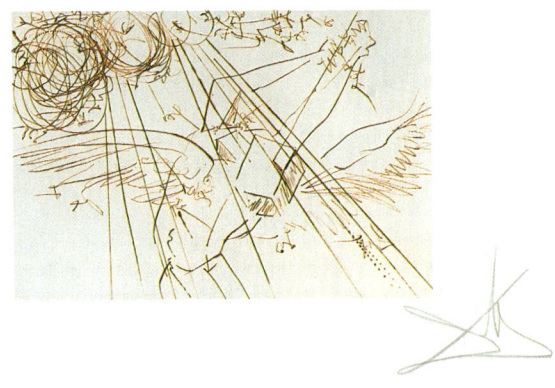

SUPPLEMENT

A FEW LETTERS FROM NIKOS KAZANTZAKIS TO KIMON FRIAR[1]

1. Kimon Friar in "The Medusa,"[2] Poros, Greece

Villa Manolita
Antibes
July 1, 1951

Dear friend,

.... What did I want to express in the *Odyssey*? The only answer is: whatever I expressed in my *Spiritual Exercises*,[3] my "Credo." But in regard to this Prevelakis[4] can explain better than I. Because, as you know, a poet knows less about his work than a good reader. Ghika also knows the *Odyssey* well, and whatever he says carries weight. Best of all would be, if at all possible, for us to meet; it would give me great joy to receive you here in my home where you may remain for as many days as you like, for it now seems to me rather difficult to come to Greece in the near future. I would very much like to help you and to speak to you about the *Odyssey*, in which I have placed all my sorrows, my joys, my struggles, and my salvation. But I find it difficult to speak about myself; perhaps if we meet, and an "atmosphere of confession" is created between us, I shall be able to speak. I am happy to know that you have the *Odyssey*, that you are reading it, and that you want to translate a few of its verses. One day perhaps I shall be able to realize my keenest desire: to see all of it translated into English free verse; it's the only language which can render it with concentration and brilliance.

Yours,
N. Kazantzakis

---

[1] Taken from about a hundred letters, twenty-two of which, including these, have appeared in "A Unique Collaboration; Translating *The Odyssey: A Modern Sequel*" by Kimon Friar, *Journal of Modern Literature* (*Nikos Kazantzakis Special Number*), 2.2 (1971–1972); 215–244.

[2] The name of Friar's cottage on the island of Poros in the Saronic Gulf, named after a collage of Medusa made for him by the Greek artist Nikos Hadjikyriakos-Ghika and imbedded into the wall above the lintel of the front door. It was Ghika who first introduced Friar to the *Odyssey*; his thirty-five illustrations for the poem appear in *The Odyssey: A Modern Sequel* (New York: Simon and Schuster, 1958).

2. Kimon Friar in Athens

Antibes
April 16, 1955

Dear Kimon,

I have found time at last to look at your[5] translation line by line, and now send you a note on very few things.

I derived great joy from reading your translation; it is not a translation but a recreation. Your strength, your language, and your rhythm is a great accomplishment. It seems to me that at times you surpass the original, and I thank you very much. No one in the entire world could have done anything better for me; if the *Odyssey* is ever to be saved, I shall owe it to you, because it would go unjustly lost if it remained in Greek. May your heart remain always as healthy and warm as it is, and your mind always luminous. Let's hope that I, too, shall remain in health that I may live to see the *Odyssey* published in English. . . .

I have only this to tell you: what great happiness Book I gave me, what a miracle your work is. I'm now waiting for Book II. I wonder when the time will come when I shall be writing you: I'm waiting for Book XXIV?

I clasp your hands with love and gratitude.

N. Kazantzakis

How much I should have liked to have heard your talks! Many have written me that they were superb. Will you publish them perhaps?[6] . . . We miss you here very much during these beautiful and sunwashed days.

Health and joy and strength and love,

N.

---

[3] See *The Saviors of God: Spiritual Exercises* by Nikos Kazantzakis, translated with an Introduction by Kimon Friar (New York: Simon and Schuster, 1961).

[4] Pandelis Prevelakis, Greek author and friend of the poet. See his *Nikos Kazantzakis and His Odyssey: A Study of the Poet and the Poem*, translated by Philip Sherrard with a Preface by Kimon Friar (New York: Simon and Schuster, 1961).

[5] During their collaboration, and in his letters to Friar afterward, Kazantzakis always addressed Friar in the familiar singular. An extraordinarily shy man, he rarely addressed anyone in the singular, not even his dearest friend, Prevelakis, nor his beloved wife, Helen.

[6] Kazantzakis is referring to an earlier version of the talk which has finally seen publication in these pages, and which in earlier versions Friar delivered in many parts of Greece, both in English and in Greek.

3. Kimon Friar in Athens

Antibes
June 6, 1955

My dear Kimon,

Conqueror of Crete! What an upheaval you have caused! What a triumph that was, and how wonderfully you have conquered our great island with your words! I have read all the newspapers you sent me . . . and I've received a flood of letters that tell me how beautifully you spoke, how deeply you moved all the Cretans, and how, wherever you went, you saw and conquered.

I am deeply happy because in this way our two names will be joined so fraternally and with such splendor. With deep emotion I have read your letter many times where you recount everything so well. And I am happy that you have become friends with my nephew Nikos and with all my relatives. The photographs are superb, but I cannot recognize my paternal home; it has become a ruin, and my sister a ruin also, who was such a beautiful girl in her youth. I do not fear death, I loathe the body's decline. . . .

All during these days Helen and I have been talking about your triumphal campaign in Crete, and our happiness and emotion is profound. There is no such thing as chance, there is only Destiny; for it was fated that you should come from America and that you should have found in your youth what I discovered only after much struggle; and that we should be agreed on the greatest and most basic problems of man, his fate, and his art. I am positive that you will go beyond the summit where I have stopped, and that you will proceed much further. You have what I lack, and in particular you have youth. I am happy that I will now die in peace because I shall leave on this earth a man younger and better than I.

All this gives me great happiness — I think that for a spiritual man no greater happiness exists.

May you be well always,
                  I thank you and clasp your hand,
                                  N. Kazantzakis

4. Kimon Friar at "The Medusa," Poros, Greece

Antibes
August 23, 1955

Our dear Kimon,

. . . I want one thing only: that the translation be done by you, because only thus may I be certain that the translation can become even better than the original. My happiness when I read your English verses is very great. Only your collaboration can render whatever beauty there is in the *Odyssey*. . . . I want one thing only: that the translation be completed as soon as possible in order that I may live long enough to see it and take joy in it.[7] . . . I am still receiving letters from everywhere in Greece describing with what joy and emotion everyone listened to your words on the *Odyssey*. In the parched provinces of Greece your words fell like the first spring rain. . . . You must know this: that you are my greatest hope.

> Always
> N. Kazantzakis

5. Kimon Friar at "The Medusa," Poros, Greece

> [Antibes]
> September 12, 1955

My Dear Kimon,

. . . The work is great and difficult, and only you in the world can do it to perfection; for this reason we both must do whatever we can that it may be completed quickly and well. I have written you, and I repeat: *you are my last hope.*[8] . . .

What happiness it would be if you could pass through Antibes on your way to America. We would talk and we would agree on everything. You would give us inexpressible joy. You now belong to us: I would never have accepted any other son but you.[9] Our meeting in that Florentine villa had a deep meaning. I had guessed it immediately; but now I am certain. Keep my love, dear Kimon, and keep well.

> N. Kazantzakis

6. Kimon Friar in Athens

> Antibes
> February 2, 1956

Beloved, immortal Kimon,

You can't imagine with what joy I received your new verses. I see that you are able to work now,[10] that the holy rhythm has once more entered

---

[7] Kazantzakis lived to see and verify the complete translation, but died a year before its publication. His untimely death also robbed him of the Nobel Prize in Literature.

[8] These last words were written in English.

[9] He was childless.

[10] Friar had broken his leg in a motorcycle accident, had been hospitalized, and was now convalescing.

into your life, that you have once more plunged into the deathless waters of poetry. No other salvation exists, no other reality exists — only Poetry. May you be well, the evil has passed, the holy Ascent begins again.

Not a moment passes that I do not bring you into my mind and heart; this world is a mystery, and mysterious the chemical affinities between men. I always think it a great joy that we two met on this beloved crust of earth.

I work, as always, as though I have over my head a master, a boss, with a whip in his hand. What shall we call this boss? God? Certainly not; let's say that he is the highest Summit of our souls.

Health, joy, and a good meeting!

N. Kazantzakis

7. Kimon Friar in Melrose Park, Illinois

Antibes
June 5, 1957

Dear Kimon,

In a few hours we shall leave for Berne-Moscow-China. Much confusion; I hope that everything will turn out well.

You are in America now, and God knows when we shall receive a letter from you to find out what you've done, how you are, how the New World seems to you, and how you found your family.

We shall both write you from Moscow and China, but where can you write us? Perhaps we can send you some address when we arrive there.

We think of you all the time and ask ourselves when we shall see you again. There's a possibility that we may come to America; I must not leave this earth without seeing you, before I see the work you have in mind, that I may rejoice in it. I am writing you hurriedly, in the midst of luggage. Again I am taking the road to insanity which has always been for me the road to the highest wisdom.

A good encounter, Kimon!

N. Kazantzakis

8. Kimon Friar in Melrose Park

Illustrated postcard of a bird perched on a blossoming cherry bough.

Peking
June 24, 1957

Dear Kimon,

What can you be doing? When shall we receive a letter from you? We shall be in Yugoslavia in August. We bring you to mind, into our hearts, every moment. You would like the yellow world here very much. I force my body to obey my soul, and thus I never tire. We shall return to Europe via the North Pole. I am saying farewell to all things, all things are saying their farewell to me. Nevermore.[11] The fairy tale is coming to an end.

               Love,
                      Nikos

---

[11] In English.

CRITICAL COMMENT ON *THE ODYSSEY: A MODERN SEQUEL*

These selections are culled from over one hundred and sixty reviews and articles that have appeared in the United States and England on the publication of Kazantzakis' *The Odyssey: A Modern Sequel* as translated by Kimon Friar. The selections, condensed, were chosen on the basis of their source, whether periodical or newspaper, and on the ability of the critic to judge as poet, writer, editor, translator, or specialist in the field of Classical or Modern Greek studies.

CECIL MAURICE BOWRA, Greek Scholar, Vice-Chancellor of Oxford University, editor of *The Oxford Book of Ancient Greek Verse*, author of *The Greek Experience*, etc. In *The London Observer*, Sunday, Feb. 8, 1959. "In our time a most remarkable epic has been composed and is now presented in an English version hardly less remarkable. Nikos Kazantzakis was one of the select band of writers, like Tolstoy, Hardy, Rilke, and Conrad, who escaped the notice of the electors to the Nobel Prize. His novels are among the most impressive of our time, but his most astonishing and original creation was his epic *Odyssey*. Such a book called for translation, but until Mr. Friar undertook the heroic task, it seemed unlikely that anyone would have the necessary knowledge, accomplishment, and courage to do it.

Mr. Friar's translation is a great achievement. He has reduced the line to twelve or thirteen syllables [from seventeen], and this is about as many as an English line can take. . . . He is scrupulously careful and accurate, understands the poem from inside, and has made it part of himself. His translation reads like an original work, and yet he had added nothing to what he has found in the Greek. He has caught the tense, passionate, varied tone of Kazantzakis without falling into rhetoric or flatness.

[Kazantzakis has fused in Odysseus] a single Titanic character who seems to carry on his shoulders the fortunes of the human race and to embody its lowest and its highest characteristics. Yet though Kazantzakis's Odysseus is a great deal larger than life, and several times as natural, he is indisputably alive in his zest for action and danger, his powerful appetites, his searching curiosity, his desire to find out the inner meaning of existence, his love of life and his gradual discovery of what really matters most in it.

The story is of fascinating interest for its own sake. Kazantzakis was not a novelist for nothing, and the bold invention which gives such strength to his novels is at work in his *Odyssey*. The episodes are as exciting, unusual, dramatic and disturbing as we can wish, and we can never forecast what will happen next."

In a letter to the publishers, Simon and Schuster, about the translation:

"A most masterly performance. Both a great memorial to a great man and a most notable work of art in itself. Kimon Friar has really caught the spirit and tone of the original, especially its concentrated power and fullness. This is one of the hardest things in the world to do, and he has done it with consummate skill. Nobody can now say it is impossible to know what Kazantzakis is like without knowing Greek, for Mr. Friar has given a real and true impression of it. But he has also created a work of art in its own right. In his English translation this great poem stands on its own strength and has no weak spots or failures to sustain its tone. I have been in bed and read it slowly and carefully and was continually delighted not only by its faithfulness to the original but by its strength and independence. It is a great achievement, and the great poet would be delighted."

MOSES HADAS, Jay Professor of Greek and Latin, Columbia University, author of *A History of Greek Literature*, etc. Front page of the *New York Herald Tribune Book Review*, December 7, 1958. "A stirring work of art, a major achievement. Its enormous sweep justifies its spaciousness and its concentrations demand its own energetic mode of discourse. Character, incident, and background, alike intense and passionate and sensual, are credible and absorbing enough to engage interest for the narrative alone, but the contrapuntal technique, the ironies and ambiguities and evocations, enfold layers of meaning . . . This *Odyssey* is valid as a poem because it is more economical as well as more effective than prose could be. It would not be, for the English reader, were it not for the extraordinary skill of Mr. Kimon Friar's admirable version. To hit the right vernacular tone where bookishness would be a distortion, to reproduce the brevity of ambivalence and especially of gnomic utterance where expansion would be fatal, and to match Kazantzakis's own strength in melodious and effortless verses without flagging through a poem longer than the *Iliad* and the *Odyssey* combined is no small feat."

DUDLEY FITTS, teacher of English at Phillips Academy, Greek Scholar, translator of *The Birds, Antigone, Oedipus at Colonus, Oedipus the King, Alcestis, The Frogs, Agamemnon*, etc. Front page of the *New York Times Book Review*, Dec. 7, 1958. "A superb and enormous poem . . . Congratulations are in order, but how shall we apportion them? Chiefly, to Kimon Friar, of course, for a labor that is itself of epic dimensions . . . Of Mr. Friar's translation I can only say that it reads magnificently. An accomplished poet himself, he knows exactly how to achieve the freshness of diction and cadence that distinguishes poetry from fustian, good translation from indifferent. His taste is nearly faultless. One can only gaze with admiration at passage after passage of noble eloquence, and of elevation that transcends action and enters the regions of glory. A high argument greatly argued."

EDITH HAMILTON, Professor of Greek at Bryn Mawr College, author of *The Greek Way*, Honorary Citizen of Athens. In a letter to the publishers March, 25, 1959: "I refer to Kimon Friar's book, and I do so advisedly, for it will never be read, in my opinion, as a translation. Its extraordinary success leaves no room for regret; I know of no other translator who has been acclaimed as a poet in his own right."

JAMES A. NOTOPOULOS, Professor of Classics, Trinity College, Hartford, Conn., author of *Modern Greek Heroic Oral Poetry*, etc. In *The Virginia Quarterly Review*, Spring, 1959. "Kazantzakis' epic is unique in giving the epic a sweep, a titanic enlargement and dimensions never seen before in the epic. In this he is at the opposite extreme of Joyce's *Ulysses*, who confines the dimensions of his world to a petty day spent in Dublin. Epic sweep is the sustained tempo of Kazantzakis' epic; titanic objectives of the human spirit, titanic space co-ordinates in geography, history, and philosophy are ever present. This hugeness of form is dictated by the daemonic obsession of Kazantzakis' hero to use the human spirit to burst through the time-space limits of the Greek world, to destroy old and rotten civilizations such as Crete and Egypt, to build new ones in the heart of Africa. . . . Like Homer's Titans, who piled Pelion on Ossa to scale Olympos, so our hero confounds the traditional planes of man and god, destroys the outworn gods and enthrones the human mind as the new divinity. . . .

This is surely a strange Odysseus. Homer's denizen of Ithaca encounters gods, sleeps with goddesses, yet he still stays within the mortal bounds of the golden mean — there is man and there is god. For Kazantzakis there is no golden mean, only golden extremes. Man is god, did he realize his own divinity and the shadowy quality of time, space, Fate, the gods, even Death. Here is a humanism that has never before been articulated with such extremes.

Whereas Joyce manipulates the Odyssey myth to depict the anarchy and futility of modern life, Kazantzakis manipulates it to depict the splendor and potentialities of the human spirit. In this he is far closer to the Greek tradition as well as to the poetic intent of Homer himself. Thus one of the by-products of this translation will be to offer students of contemporary literature an exercise in the contrasted usage and the rich potentialities of the mythical method to mirror the human spirit in its diverse moods.

Kimon Friar is to be congratulated on the translation. Wherever I have sampled his version with the Greek text of Kazantzakis, it reveals a poet translating a poet. His introduction and notes enhance the poem as a scholarly edition."

GILBERT HIGHET, Professor of Classics, Columbia University, author of *The Classical Tradition*, etc. In *The Book-of-the-Month* transcript of a radio talk given over the National Broadcasting Company and 100 affiliated stations: "Mystics, poets, revolutionaries, Greek-Americans, pantheists, philhellenes, classicists, eroticists, and other-worldists should buy this book and begin to read it slowly and with relish . . . The poetry (so far as I can judge from the translation) is remarkably original and stirring. From the first page to the last it is packed with imagery. The images are often mixed and incongruous; the poet does not care, for he hates logic and loves the hyperbolic and the impossible. But they are nearly always boldly original.

The emotions are as intense and improbable as the images. If you have read Kazantzakis' novels, you will recall how his heroes are fabulously strong, prodigious drinkers and desperate fighters, supermen careless of convention and immune to fatigue, Herculean lovers: one of them breaks three beds on his wedding night. The same is true of the characters in his *Odyssey*: they lust and fight and travel and starve and laugh more like Titans than like men; their battles are equal to the fiercest Homeric combats or the great adventures of the modern Greek *palikári*, and their sensual passions outdo anything in the tamer life of classical Greece. Furthermore, the entire poem is studded by dreams, and fables, and symbols, and visions (some of them inspired by wild Greek folklore) which takes us even further out of the frontiers of reality. To read this poem is to go out on a voyage of exploration, into the unknown and the unimagined.

But, you will ask, what does this all lead to? As we thread our way through the dense maze of symbolism which fills the central and later books, we see that Odysseus is an exceptional human soul in search of truth. He passes through all these experiences and savors them, to find out whether through them he can understand life. He rejects first one solution after another, but he goes on experimenting until his death. . . . The *Odyssey* of Kazantzakis, therefore, is a spiritual epic. In poetry, it belongs to the same class as the *Divine Comedy* of Dante, Goethe's *Faust*, and the poem of the neglected Swiss genius, Karl Spitteler, called *Olympian Spring*."

ANDONIS DECAVALLES, Poet, translator into Greek of T. S. Eliot's *Four Quartets*, Professor of Comparative Literature, Fairleigh Dickinson University, Madison, New Jersey. In *Poetry*, Chicago, 1959. "This modern epic is undoubtedly the greatest long poem of our time, a colossal achievement in art and substance. It is the mature product of Kazantzakis' deep familiarity with the best in world literature and thought, of intense living, traveling, and thinking. . . . Odysseus never ceases to be the supreme embodiment of Greece, its spirit of an unfailing faith in life and freedom, of enrichment and rebirth through ever new experiences. Yet the range in which Odysseus shapes and fulfills his destiny in this new poem is far wider than when he gave us his old, Homeric report. Three thousand years of further physical and spiritual exploration have passed since then.

Ithaca is not now the hero's own soul, the fulfillment of his own being, a full self-conquest as the supreme gain. What appears as progress through rejections is really a progress through conquests and affirmations. Life is good and Death is good. The mirror power of the Quest is fire, the Sun, God, clarity, man's burning body and heart and mind, wherein all things become one and priceless, where all antitheses merge into a universal synthesis. What a precious message of love to come in our time of disparity, what warm affirmation of life, not unrealistic, for a world of anxiety, bitterness, disaffection, frenzied rejection or predilection. For the partial, here is the complete man offered, powerful and integral, able to create his own fate against Fate, his Manhood above God.

Kimon Friar deserves unstinted praise for his achievement in the translation of this poem. It was a colossal undertaking for which the least thing to praise would be the extraordinary amount of dedication involved. His precise scholarship, but more, his own poetic gift, has enabled him to produce what must be considered an English Masterpiece. He has made the best possible choice of his expressive media, the English iambic hexemeter, to preserve and recreate whatever could be preserved and recreated from the original."

MAURICE DOLBIER, Critic, in *The New York Herald Tribune*, Dec. 6, 1958. Generation after generation of literary scholars will explore the style and sources of this epic, while other students will investigate its religious and philosophical meanings, and other poets will draw inspiration from it for their own works. Like Shakespeare and *Don Quixote*, Proust and *Faust*, Joyce and *Moby Dick*, and the works of the writer of the first *Odyssey*, it is a book that takes root in the mind of man and grows and grows there. . . . It is a wonderful story full of strange adventures on land, sea, and in the brain and bloodstream. What no outline can suggest is the spellbinding nature of the poem, its richness of metaphor, its sensuousness, its joy in the variousness and the simplicities of life, its rapidity of pace, its bursting imaginativeness. Through Kimon Friar's translation, a foreign masterwork has become an English masterwork."

JOHN CIARDI, Poet, Poetry Editor of *Saturday Review*. In *Saturday Review*, cover review, Dec. 13, 1958. "*The Odyssey: A Modern Sequel* is not a book of the year, nor a book of the decade, but a monument of the age. [A poem] of true majesty, an epic of Homeric stature. Kimon Friar has produced an English version that stamps him as a master translator in his own right."

CLIFTON FADIMAN, Member of the Board of Directors of the Encyclopaedia Britanica, editor of *The Life-Time Reading Plan*, *The American Treasury*, etc. In *The Book of the Month Club News*, 1958. "*The Odyssey: A Modern Sequel* is Nikos Kazantzakis' masterpiece. It is offered to English and American readers in a translation by Kimon Friar of remarkable beauty and energy, with a style uniquely and confidently its own. A remarkable tour de force. Kazantzakis' *magnum opus* may in time be ranked as far more than that. It has burning vitality and copiousness of imagination, and behind every line one seems to feel the force of a major personality." In a broadcast over the Columbia National Company, Dec. 28, 1958: "If I were to choose the book of the year which seems to me to have the stature of a great classic and which may indeed be remembered when you and I are no more, I would choose *The Odyssey: A Modern Sequel.*"

MAX GISSEN, Book Review Editor, *Time Magazine*, for Dec. 8, 1958. "Masterpieces of literature are hard to come by and even harder to recognize. But in *The Odyssey: A Modern Sequel*, chances are that U.S. readers have a masterpiece at hand, in a fine translation . . . The poem is a huge repository of bloody adventure, eroticism, brutal sights and sounds, magnificent descriptions of the earth, sea, and sky, and all their wonders. Man's coarsest appetites and his noblest aspirations exist side by side in Odysseus, and he is as ready to seduce a simple girl by pretending to be a god as he is to admit his doubts about himself and the human condition. This is a book of singular power and beauty. Translator Kimon Friar received from Kazantzakis the ultimate praise: that the translation was as good as the original."

ARTHUR MILLER, Playwright, author of *Death of a Salesman, The Crucible*, etc. Letter to the publishers: "In reading *The Odyssey: A Modern Sequel*, one feels that this continuation has lain in the womb of time all these centuries, and that of course it must now be shown to the world, but it has always been *there*. This epic has a genuine rhythm of its own; there is something sea-like in its pulse, in the timing of its events and their appearances. And best of all, Odysseus *is* that thing, not quite a man and yet capable of arousing the feelings reserved for things human in us. The poem is a great achievement."

W. B. STANFORD, Regius Professor of Greek, Trinity College, Dublin University, author of *The Ulysses Theme*, editor of *The Odyssey of Homer*, etc. "This is more than a magnificent, half-picaresque, half-symbolical story. It is a poem of unusual, at times monstrous beauty in diction, imagery and rhythm. Mr. Friar's translation is an amazing achievement, especially when we remember how Homer's much simpler *Odyssey* has suffered from unfaithful or incompetent translators. His greatest merit is the sustained buoyancy and flexibility of his style throughout his gigantic task. . . . Metrists will find stimulating new materials in his discussion of rhythms. Few authors have been so fortunate as Kazantzakis in having a poet, scholar, and disciple as their first translator.

The bigger the work of art, the longer the tradition behind it, the harder it is to see it in a true perspective. Quantitatively there is no doubt that this is the largest version of the *Odyssey* ever made. And qualitatively? It will take a generation of readers and critics to decide this. The present writer can only say that after a long study it still seems to rank with Joyce's *Ulysses* as one of the great literary achievements of this century both as development of the traditional Ulysses theme and — what matters much more — as a work of creative imagination." *Encounter*, July 1959, Vol. XIII, No. 1.

HUGH LLOYD JONES, Professor of Greek, Oxford University. In *The Spectator*, London, March 6, 1959. "This *Odyssey* is no pastiche of Homer, but a modern work of the highest originality and poetic power. This Odysseus is a born adventurer, a romantic realist, remarkable not for mere cunning but for physical and moral strength and courage and for a restless urge to win salvation by exploring to the root his soul's relation to God and to the universe. The work is, above all, a religious poem, a record of the search for the understanding of God and the universe; but it is as far removed as possible from the bloodless aridity of most symbolical writing. Just as the writer's mysticism insists on the acceptance of the universe, so does his poetry describe life in the world in all its concreteness with tremendous realism and power. The Odysseus of Kazantzakis goes beyond most other contemplatives in pressing forward to the last victory over Hope, the willing acceptance of annihilation. We are reminded of how the ancient poets of his race faced, without an instant of false self-consolation, the ultimate facts of human impotence and mortality; and we see the link that connects the greatest Greek poem of modern times with the sublime acceptance of man's fate that concludes Pindar's last and greatest ode of victory.

This great poem presented a most formidable problem to the translator; but the problem has been triumphantly surmounted by Mr. Kimon Friar . . . But it is clear that Mr. Friar himself is a poet of unusual gifts. He has performed the amazing feat of presenting a vast epic narrative in clear, vigorous and beautiful English which steers a successful course between the whirlpools of modern vulgarism and the dead shallows of traditional versifying. Kazantzakis, with sure poetic instinct, eschewed the traditional 'political meter' with its monotonous beat in favor of a seventeen-syllable iambic measure which allowed him to achieve a wholly new variety of rhythm. Mr. Friar has skillfully reproduced the effect of this by using an 'iambic hexameter' which stands to the traditional English pentameter rather as Kazantzakis' meter does to the traditional Greek line of fifteen syllables, and the explanation of his metrical principles deserves careful study by everyone interested in modern English verse technique."

PATRICK LEIGH FERMOR, author of *Mani, Roumeli*, translator of *The Cretan Runner*. In *The Sunday London Times*, Feb. 8, 1959. "It becomes compellingly clear that if the word 'genius' has any meaning, Kazantzakis was one. The appearance of his *Odyssey* here is a major literary event. The poem is a long search for a private solution to the underlying chaos of life, to the breakdown of systems; the search for the maximum fulfillment of man's role in the evolutionary chain. The spirit of the later Yeats is not absent. But what remains uppermost for the reader at the end of this long journey is the boldness and vigor and beauty of the poetry. It tunnels, gallops, soars, floats, explodes, sinks in golden rain, reforms. Suns swoop and rotate. Tendrils twirl, leaves put forth and fall, pulses beat. We, like the devious, city-sacking, curious, thoughtful and lonely king have crossed dark woods, risen from flickering alcoves and stalked bloody-handed down the corridors of palaces and held the tiller across tempestuous hexametric seas. We must here salute Kimon Friar's translation; his fascinating but daunting task has been majestically fulfilled. Mr. Friar has skillfully, almost miraculously, captured the force, the originality, the fire, the bite and the splendour of the original."

IAN SCOTT-KILVERT, Modern Greek Scholar. Member of the Board of the British Institute, Athens, translator of Plutarch's *Nine Greek Lives*. In *The Daily Telegraph*, London, Feb. 13, 1959. "Kimon Friar has achieved an extraordinary feat in reproducing so much of the metrical vigour and the riotous exhuberance of the poet's expression. The total effect is of a poem magnificent in its vision of man and nature, but unwieldy in design. Kazantzakis caries away the reader with the boldness of his thought and the opulence of his images. While many writers have narrowed the character of Odysseus, Kazantzakis has immensely enlarged it. As in his other books, he deliberately yokes a soaring idealism with a grotesque, often brutal sensuality. For this Odysseus there is no problem of temptation: his destiny is to explore the furthest bounds of human experience, sensual, intellectual, and spiritual. Kazantzakis has often shocked those who demand tranquillity and order in all things Greek; he has built his epic, for it is nothing less, not on despair, but on the harsh, unresolved complexity of modern experience. He wrote it in the conviction which most artists of his age have shared, that a serene art, secure in its assumptions, is behind us, and possibly before us, but certainly not with us."

E. V. RIEU, Professor of Classics, editor of The Penguin Classic series, translator of Homer's *Odyssey*. In a letter to the Publisher, May 11, 1959: "I began reading *The Odyssey: A Modern Sequel* with great qualms. I am one of those who believe that Odysseus is better left to Homer — I grudge him even to Dante. But as I read on, I began to feel that Nikos Kazantzakis had conceived a great poem which could stand in its own right. Wherever one opens the book, one finds new and original poetry. How much is due to Kimon Friar's masterly translation? Not knowing the original, I cannot answer. All I can say is that I am filled with admiration for his great skill."

JAMES DICKEY, former Consultant in Poetry to the Library of Congress, author of *Poems 1957–1967*. In *The Sewanee Review*, Summer, 1959. "Nikos Kazantzakis' *The Odyssey: A Modern Sequel* appears among all other contemporary poetry as an elemental force of nature than as a 'work of art,' or as a thing that can be bound between the covers of a book. In sheer force of invention, in its primitive, unleashed, fleshly splendor and a kind of gluttonous ravening over the world of the senses, it is unmatched by anything I have ever read, long and involved as it is . . . Though they are frequently over-long, and there are a great many of them, the countless soliloquies, asides, dreams, and digressions do, in actuality, but little to impede the wild barbaric onrushing of the narrative from scene to scene, from place to place, from event to event, as Odysseus and his followers plunge through a gorgeously sensuous world which matches the hero's own tremendous animal vitality as well as his moments of reflection and the turns of his 'many-sided mind.' The feeling of life extravagantly, deeply, and meaningfully lived is in every line of the poem; not only are the personages unforgettably vivid, down to the least slave serving wine in a harbor tavern, but the very objects of the poem seem to have an independent life of their own, too: swords, shields, the robes of women, the stones on the road, the stars above the ship all pulsate with uniqueness, mystery, beauty, and immediacy, so that the reader realizes, time after time, how very little he has himself been willing to settle for, in living: how much there *is* upon earth: how wild, inexplicable, marvelous, and endless creation is. The real effect of Kazantzakis' immense poem is to bring forward (and with unbelievable fullness!) the incalculable value of a total response to experience. The greatest tribute I can pay the poet is to say that his grafting of various symbols onto the actions of his hero soon falls into a kind of secondary or parallel interest, and that the prime fascination of the poem comes out of Kazantzakis' tumultuously vital evocation of the physical world itself, apprehended in a joyously primitive splendor that dazzles, dazes, and finally overwhelms the reader with his own admiration and gratitude.

When one looks back over Kazantzakis' *Odyssey* and recalls its thousands of vivid details as well as its irresistibly forceful major passages . . . one sees that one has had part in what is likely the most remarkable sustained accomplishment in verse that the modern imagination has been privileged to record. When one notes, too, that this huge, questing hymn to daring and fecundity has been written, not at all in a Miltonic striving for 'greatness,' but in the most intense and personal creative joy, one is but the more impressed, and the more indebted to both poet and translator. . . .

The final good of the new *Odyssey*, I suspect, will not be to glorify the Nietzschean hero, or make aesthetically viable the ideas of Bergson, Nietzsche, or Spengler, or even 'man's dauntless mind,' but to restore the sense of the heedless delight in living to a jaded populace. To poets it is, and it will be a living demonstration of the profound vitality that words may be made to carry by a poet who is himself profoundly vital, and of the human power that makes the best poetry nearly as valuable as life. It shows, also, that this power, at its most significant issues, not tentatively and fraught with contingencies, but directly and unalterably from the deepest, unanalysed springs of the personality. It is this power which appropriates the forms of writing and uses them to create and explore new realms of the imagination, and ultimately to establish them, so that they may become the most enduring ground of the spirit. In this connection, Odysseus is likely to prove a hero to us in more ways than even his chronicler has envisioned, and Kazantzakis himself in all ways."

MARVIN LOWENTHAL, Director of Special Services, Brandeis University Library, in a letter to the publishers, July 20, 1959. "The ghosts of other poets and thinkers lend a breath to Kazantzakis' sails: Dante, who also wrecked Ulysses in the southern ocean; Tennyson, who sent him West rather than South and, in a nobler touch, left him alive and forever steering onward. There are overtones — for the theme is universal — of Faust's quest, of Flaubert's Saint Anthony, of Nectaire's tale in France's *Revolt of the Angels*, of H. G. Wells' God-in-the-making, of a swish from Frazier's Golden Bough, and even of the sword-swaggerer Jurgen. But the big wind, the gigantic billowing voyage is altogether Kazantzakis' own. His *Odyssey* will rank among the greatest achievements of modern poetry.

Sometimes, indeed rather often, there is too much of a good thing. But this is a defect apparently inseparable from the exuberance of genius: there is too much of *Faust, The Divine Comedy,* and *Don Quixote.* No law, fortunately, requires a man to read Kazantzakis all at one go. Each major episode taken separately, and read — as I have done — at a leisurely pace — has the merits and rewards of a major narrative poem throbbing with excitement and beauty.

For the beauty we have to rely, of course, on the translation, itself something of a marvel — Mr. Friar makes the Greek poet sound as though he had written directly in English. The translation as such vanishes — which is the acme of the translatory art. There are dozens of happy phrases and epithets, of haunting turns of speech, which would make the fortune of a contemporary English poet. I should like to hear Mr. Friar sing out in his own voice."

MARY RENAULT, author of novels on ancient Greece: *The Last of the Wine, The King Must Die, The Bull from the Sea, The Mask of Apollo, Fire from Heaven.* "One of this century's major imaginative achievements. As one reads, all the affinities that suggest themselves are gigantic: the magnificent decoration, the compressed images, the splendid despair are Elizabethan, sometimes almost Shakespearean; but the flow and surge of the whole, with its rhythm which suggest that of natural forces, wind or sea, has echoes of Blake; and in its apocalyptic visions of natural disaster and human catastrophe Melville would recognize a congenial element. One cannot but feel oneself in the presence of a noble integrity and an unflinching courage. . . . The translation reads like an original work, and one is not surprised to hear that Kazantzakis approved of it." Letter to the publisher, Dec. 7, 1958.

LAWRENCE DURRELL, author of *Prospero's Cell, Bitter Lemons, The Alexandria Quarter,* etc. In a letter to the publisher, 1958: "A poem of epic dimensions, faultlessly edited and inimitably translated."

PANAYOTIS KANELLOPOULOS, Man of Letters, former Professor at the University of Athens, former Prime Minister of Greece, in the periodical *Nea Estia*, Athens, Greece, Feb. 15,

1959. "Kazantzakis' *Odyssey* — so long as men of mind and spirit shall exist on earth — will be thought of as one of the great landmarks of our century . . . Even yesterday I would have said that it would be impossible to translate the clearly poetic and metrical work of Nikos Kazantzakis into a foreign tongue. But today I no longer have the right to say this. This English translation of the greatest epic poem of our century is so good that I am obligated to say that all true poetry may be rendered into another tongue, provided that a translator may be found who has the intellectual power and the poetic spirit of Kimon Friar.

OHIO UNIVERSITY LIBRARY